Wild Dreams
of a New Beginning

## Books by Lawrence Ferlinghetti

*A Coney Island of the Mind*
*European Poems & Transitions*
*Her*
*Routines*
*The Secret Meaning of Things*
*Starting from San Francisco*
*These Are My Rivers. New & Selected Poems 1955-1993*
*A Trip to Italy and France*
*Wild Dreams of a New Beginning*

Lawrence Ferlinghetti

# Wild Dreams of a New Beginning

A New Directions Book

Manufactured in the United States of America.
New Directions Books are printed on acid-free paper.
First published clothbound and as New Directions Paperback 663 in
1988.
Published simultaneously in Canada by Penguin Books Canada Limited.

Publisher's note: *Wild Dreams of a New Beginning* combines two
earlier New Directions editions, *Who Are We Now?* (1976) and
*Landscapes of Living & Dying* (1979).

Library of Congress Cataloging-in-Publication Data
Ferlinghetti, Lawrence.
    [Who are we now]
    Wild dreams of a new beginning / Lawrence Ferlinghetti.
        p.       cm.    A New Directions Book
    Contents: Who are we now?—Landscapes of living & dying.
    ISBN 0-8112-1074-X    ISBN 0-8112-1075-8 (pbk.)
        I. Ferlinghetti, Lawrence. Landscapes of living & dying.    1988.
II. Title.
PS3511.E557W5    1988                                    88-5304
811'.54—dc 19                                            CIP

New Directions Books are published for James Laughlin
by New Directions Publishing Corporation,
80 Eighth Avenue, New York 10011.

FIFTH PRINTING

# CONTENTS

## WHO ARE WE NOW?

## LANDSCAPES OF LIVING & DYING

# WILD DREAMS OF A NEW BEGINNING

# WHO ARE WE NOW?

"Underneath all art and social life, sex and fraternity"
—Edward Carpenter, *Days with Walt Whitman*

# THE JACK OF HEARTS
(*For Dylan*)

Who are we now, who are we ever,
Skin books parchment bodies libraries of the living
gilt almanachs of the very rich
encyclopedias of little people
packs of players face down
on faded maps of America
with no Jack of Hearts
in the time of the ostrich
Fields full of rooks
dumb pawns in black-and-white kingdoms
And revolutions the festivals of the oppressed
and festivals the little revolutions
of the bourgeoisie
where gypsy fortune tellers deal
without the Jack of Hearts
the black-eyed one who sees all ways
the one with the eye of a horse
the one with the light in his eye
the one with his eye on the star named Nova
the one for the ones with no one to lead them
the one whose day has just begun
the one with the star in his cap
the cat with future feet
looking like a Jack of Hearts
mystic Jack Zen Jack with crazy koans
Vegas Jack who rolls the bones
the high roller behind the dealer
the one who'll shake them
the one who'll shake the ones unshaken
the fearless one

the one without bullshit
the stud with the straightest answer
the one with blazing words for guns
the distance runner with the word to pass
the night rider with the urgent message
The man from La Mancha riding bareback
The one who bears the great tradition
and breaks it
The Mysterious Stranger who comes & goes
The Jack of Hearts who speaks out
in the time of the ostrich
the one who sees the ostrich
the one who sees what the ostrich sees in the sand
the one who digs the mystery
and stands in the corner smiling
like a Jack of Hearts
at the ones with no one to lead them
the ones with their eyes in the sands
the sand that runs through the glass
the ones who don't want to look
at what's going down around them
the shut-eye ones who wish
that someone else would seize the day
that someone else would tell them
which way up and which way out
and whom to hate and whom to love
like Big Jack groovy Jack the Jack of light
Sainted Jack who had the Revelations
and spoke the poem of apocalypse
Poet Jack with the light pack
who travels by himself
and leaves the ladies smiling
Dharma Jack with the beatitudes
drunk on a bus addressing everyone
the silent ones with the frozen faces

the ones with *The Wall Street Journal*
who never speak to strangers
the ones that got lost in the shuffle
and never drew the Jack of Hearts
the one who'd turn them on
who'd save them from themselves
the one who heals the Hamlet in them
the silent Ham who never acts
like the Jack of Hearts
the dude on the corner in two-tone shoes
who knows the name of the game
and names his game
the kid who paints the fence
the boy who digs the treasure up
the boy with the beans on the beanstalk
the dandy man the candy man
the one with the lollipops
the harlequin man
who tells the tic-toc man to stuff it
in front of the house that Jack built
behind the house that Jack built
where sleeps the Cock that crowed in the morn
where sleeps the Cow with the crumpled horn
where sleeps the dude who kept the horse
with the beautiful form
and kissed the Maiden all forlorn
the Jack of the pack all tattered and torn
the one the queen keeps her eye on
Dark Rider on a white horse
after the Apocalypse
Prophet stoned on the wheel of fortune
Sweet singer with harp half-hid
who speaks with the cry of cicadas
who tells the tale too truly
for the ones with no one to tell them

the true tale of sound and fury
the Jack of Hearts who lays it out
who tells it as it is
the one who wears no watch
yet tells the time too truly
and reads the Knight of Cups
and knows himself
the Knave of Hearts the Jack of Hearts
who stole the tarts
of love & laughter
the Jack who tells his dream
to those with no one to dream it
the one who tells his dream
to the hard-eyed innocents
and lays it out for the blind hippie
the black dream the white dream
of the Jack of Hearts
whose skeleton is neither black nor white
the long dream the dream of heads & hearts
the trip of hearts the flip of hearts
that turns the Hanged Man right side up
and saves the Drowned Sailor
with the breath of love
the wet dream the hard dream the sweet dream
of the Deck Hand on the tall ship sailing softly
Blackjack yellowjack the steeplejack
who sets the clock in the tower
and sees the chimes of freedom flashing
his only watch within him
the high one the turned-on one the tuned-in one
the one who digs
in the time of the ostrich
and finds the sun-stone
of himself

the woman-man
the whole man
who holds all worlds together
when all is said and all is done
in the wild eye the wide eye
of the Jack of Hearts
who stands in a doorway
clothed in sun

# DIRECTOR OF ALIENATION

Looking in the mirrors at Macy's
and thinking it's a subterranean plot
to make me feel like Chaplin
snuck in with his bent shoes & beat bowler
looking for a fair-haired angel
Who's this bum
crept in off the streets
blinking in the neon
an anarchist among the floorwalkers
a strike-breaker even
right past the pickets
and the picket line is the People yet?
I think I'll hook a new derby
with my cane
and put a sign on it reading
Director of Alienation
or The Real Revolution
So it's Mister Alienation is it
like he don't like nobody?
It's not me It's Them out of step
I came in looking for an angel
male or female dark or fair
but why does everyone look
so serious or unhappy
like as if everyone's alienated
from something or someone
from the whole earth even
and the green land
among the loud indignant birds
My land is your land
but 'all is changed, changed utterly'

Look at this alien face
in this elevator mirror
The Tele-tector scans me
He looks paranoid Better get him out
before he starts trying on the underwear
Keep your filthy mitts offa
I better stick to the escalators
Too many nylon ladies in the lifts
too many two-way mirrors
I came in looking for an angel
among the alien corn
I might get caught
fingering the lingerie
feeling up the manikins
House dicks after me
Where's your credit cards
They'll find the hole in my sock
in the Shoe Department
The full-length mirrors all designed
to make you look your worst
so you'll get real depressed
and throw off your old clothes
and buy new duds on the spot
Well I'll take them at their word
They asked for it
Off with these grungy threads
and slide down the escalators bare-ass
Slip between the on-sale sheets
into the on-sale bed
feeling for an angel in it
Try this new flush toilet
and the portable shower
emerging from the bath in something sexy
into a store window
among the Coquette Wigs by Eva Gabor

and freeze in one of the wigs
when the Keystone Cops come running
I came in looking for an angel
passion eyes and longing hair
in mirrors made of water
But what's this wrack of civilization
I've fallen into
This must be the end of something
the last days of somebody's empire
Seven floors of it
from Women's Wear to Men's Furnishings
Lost souls descending thru
Dante's seven circles
Ladies like bees avaricious
clustered at counters
I don't want to join them either
Always the Outsider
What a drag
Why don't you get with it
It's your country
What a cliché this Outsider
a real bore
But is there anyone left inside
in this year of the boring Bicentennial
Indians alienated Artists alienated
All these poets alienated
Parents husbands wives alienated
Kids alienated
Even billionaires alienated
hiding out in foreign countries
Don't let them tell you different
with their flags and their grants
So Buy Buy Buy
and get Inside
Get a loada this junk

8

You wanna belong
You gotta have it
Pull yourself together
and descend to Macy's basement
And eat your way up
thru the seven stages
of this classless society
with the Credit Department on the top floor
where surely some revelation is at hand
Consume your way up
until you're consumed by it
at the very top
where surely a terrible beauty is born
Then jump off the roof
o dark of hair
o Ruth among the alien corn
waving plastic jewels and genitals

# WILD DREAMS OF A NEW BEGINNING

There's a breathless hush on the freeway tonight
Beyond the ledges of concrete
restaurants fall into dreams
with candlelight couples
Lost Alexandria still burns
in a billion lightbulbs
Lives cross lives
idling at stoplights
Beyond the cloverleaf turnoffs
'Souls eat souls in the general emptiness'
A piano concerto comes out a kitchen window
A yogi speaks at Ojai
'It's all taking place in one mind'
On the lawn among the trees
lovers are listening
for the master to tell them they are one
with the universe
Eyes smell flowers and become them
There's a deathless hush
on the freeway tonight
as a Pacific tidal wave a mile high

                                sweeps in
Los Angeles breathes its last gas
and sinks into the sea like the *Titanic* all lights lit
Nine minutes later Willa Cather's Nebraska

                                sinks with it
The seas come in over Utah
Mormon tabernacles washed away like barnacles
Coyotes are confounded & swim nowhere
An orchestra onstage in Omaha
keeps on playing Handel's *Water Music*
Horns fill with water

and bass players float away on their instruments
clutching them like lovers horizontal
Chicago's Loop becomes a rollercoaster
Skyscrapers filled like water glasses
Great Lakes mixed with Buddhist brine
Great Books watered down in Evanston
Milwaukee beer topped with sea foam
Beau Fleuve of Buffalo suddenly become salt
Manhattan Island swept clean in sixteen seconds
buried masts of Amsterdam arise
as the great wave sweeps on Eastward
to wash away over-age Camembert Europe
Mannahatta steaming in sea-vines
the washed land awakes again to wilderness
the only sound a vast thrumming of crickets
a cry of seabirds high over
in empty eternity
as the Hudson retakes its thickets
and Indians reclaim their canoes

# LOST PARENTS

It takes a fast car
                    to lead a double life
in these days of short-distance love affairs
    when he has far-out lovers in
                        three different locations
    and a date with each one
                    at least twice a week
    a little simple arithmetic shows
            what a workout he's engaged in
    crossing & recrossing the city
        from bedroom to patio to swimming pool
    the ignition key hot
        and the backseat a jumble of clothes
                        for different life-styles
    a surfboard on the roof
    and a copy of Kahlil Gibran or Rod McKuen
                    under the dashboard
        next to the Indian music casettes
    packs of Tarot and the I-Ching
                crammed into the glove compartment
        along with old traffic tickets
                    and hardpacks of Kents
        dents attesting to the passion
                        of his last lover
And his answering service
            catching him on the freeway
                between two calls or two encounter groups
    and the urgent message left
        with an unlisted number to call Carol
        about the bottle of fine wine
            he forgot to pick up
            and deliver to the gallery
                for the reception at nine

While she shuttles to her gynecologist
and will meet him later
between two other numbers
male or female
including his wife
who also called twice
wanting to know where he's been
and what he's done
with their throw-away children
who
left to their own devices
in a beach house at Malibu
grew up and dropped out into Nothing
in a Jungian search
for lost parents
their own age

# PEOPLE GETTING DIVORCED

People getting divorced
           riding around with their clothes in the car
and wondering what happened
                   to everyone and everything
                   including their other
                                   pair of shoes
           And if you spy one
               then who knows what happened
                               to the other
                                   with tongue alack
       and years later not even knowing
                       if the other ever
                           found a mate
                       without splitting the seams
                       or remained intact
                                   unlaced
       and the sole
               ah the soul
                       a curious conception
           hanging on somehow
                       to walk again
                               in the free air
                   once the heel
                               has been replaced

# SHORT STORY ON A PAINTING OF
# GUSTAV KLIMT

They are kneeling upright on a flowered bed
He
    has just caught her there
           and holds her still

   Her gown
       has slipped down
           off her shoulder

He has an urgent hunger
      His dark head
         bends to hers
           hungrily

And the woman the woman
   turns her tangerine lips from his
      one hand like the head of a dead swan
      draped down over
          his heavy neck

       the fingers
        strangely crimped
          tightly together

     her other arm doubled up
        against her tight breast
      her hand a languid claw
          clutching his hand
      which would turn her mouth
           to his

    her long dress made
        of multicolored blossoms
        quilted on gold
    her Titian hair
      with blue stars in it

And his gold
                    harlequin robe
                              checkered with
                                        dark squares
          Gold garlands
                         stream down over
                                   her bare calves &
                                        tensed feet
Nearby there must be
               a jeweled tree
                         with glass leaves aglitter
                         in the gold air
It must be
               morning
                         in a faraway place somewhere
They
     are silent together
                         as in a flowered field
               upon the summer couch
                         which must be hers
     And he holds her still
                         so passionately
               holds her head to his
                         so gently so insistently
               to make her turn
                         her lips to his
Her eyes are closed
                    like folded petals
She
     will not open
                    He
                    is not the One

# THE 'MOVING WATERS' OF
# GUSTAV KLIMT

Who are they then
              these women in this painting
             seen so deeply long ago
Models he slept with
        or lovers or others
                he came upon
    catching them as they were
              back then
       dreamt sleepers
              on moving waters
       eyes wide open
    purple hair streaming
            over alabaster bodies
      in lavender currents

Dark skein of hair blown back
             from a darkened face
      an arm flung out
          a mouth half open
       a hand
           cupping its own breast
    rapt dreamers
       or stoned realists
              drifting motionless
   lost sisters or
      women-in-love
     with themselves or others—

pale bodies wrapt
in the night of women
lapt in light
in ground swells of
dreamt desire
dreamt delight
Still strangers to us
yet not
strangers
in that first night
in which we lose ourselves

And know each other

## I AM YOU

Man half woman

Woman half man

And the two intertwined

in each of us androgynous

the limbs of one

around the limbs of the Other

clasping

my breast a vestigial remain

of yours

the heart a bivalve gasping

in a sea cave

(sound of sea waves lapping)

semen sea foam blown

into wombs of caves

thrown up

out of the body of being

out of the sea's mouth singing

19

(silent seabirds winging over)

                    And the sea incarnadine

As Saint Matthew's Passion

          sung by a blind man

                    comes over the Sunday morning radio

And I am alone here

          but if there were two of us

                    I would say

There is only one here

          in the end as in beginning

                    one body breathing

                    one body singing

And the body is us

          the body is our selves

                    and I am you

# AT THE BODEGA

The hot young stud flamenco dancer
                    dressed like a bullfighter
    has fast feet like little animals
                with their own identities
                and a life of their own
        having nothing at all to do
                    with the rest of him
            which watches
                    as they do the dancing
And each insolent gesture
                which that body makes
    and each arrogant pose
                that body takes
                    exactly like a toreador
    telling the woman he whirls around
        "I am your master
        You cannot touch me
        And in the end
        I  will bring you
        to my feet
        with this
            white handkerchief"

## SNAPSHOT EPIPHANY

One night when it was very dark
        a certain Stephen appeared to me
                        in an epiphany
                            in the Café Sport
        (that same Stephen no doubt named
            after Stephen Dedalus
                by that generation of parents
                    who named all its children
                    after the hero of
                    *Portrait of the Artist as a Young Man*)
and that same Stephen coming up to me
        with a certain subversive air
                    of an arab with a scarab
        and showing me a color photo of himself
                            in the Café Trieste
                                three years ago
            looking like a young Pierre
                in the BBC version of *War & Peace*
        and pointing out in a corner of the photo
                    'the Greek chick I'm now involved with'
            whom he hadn't even met
                        at the time of the picture
            ('The Greek *what?*' I asked him)

But there they were
                    the two of them back then
        already 'caught in the emulsion'
                    (as I pointed out to him)
            though the film not fully developed  yet
                        the final print not yet made
            the print in fact still to be
                        put back in the developer

to bring out the darker shadowed parts
                              of the total picture
in which his fated resemblance
                    to a revolutionary Pierre
        or to a liberated Stephen Dedalus
                would be made much much clearer
and her fatal resemblance
                to an Egyptian fertility goddess
                              made much dearer


even as he strides forth to forge
                'the uncreated conscience of his race'
        and even as he
                    strode back to their table
and I spied her
                through the Italian lattice
                        smiling so fatally at him
        and then kissing him
                              *gratis*

# OVERHEARD CONVERSATIONS

*(In the U.S. Restaurant & Café Sport, San Francisco, Listening to Barlow Farrar, Tony Dingman & Others)*


1.

A talent for eclectic theft
   when it came to stealing lines of poetry
    out of everybody's conversation
And Epictetus with a cactus
    couldn't have been more
      deadly with a dart
So that 'excrutia' becomes 'ex-Kruschev'
     (a Russian immigrant on the lamb)
  or another kind of Milquetoast
     with leftover spinach
      tacked to the wall
And the cardboard man in the next booth
   too 'aridite' to communicate
      with ordinary people
      with body odor
And still the whole idea of poetry being
   to take control of life
    out of the hands of
      the Terrible People


2.

And I always loved
    chance association
      she said

like a Chinese family playing mahjong
and at the same time listening to
                          Keyboard Dave
              playing the piano blues
        at Minnie's Can-Do
nonchalant as a hairdresser
              watching an assassin with a scimitar
         decapitating a heart crane
                    (a bird with  a  heart-shaped head)
And Hart Crane discovering America
         (after his father invented the lifesaver)
            by jumping from the fantail of a freighter
              in the Caribbean—
                          A pure
                          terrorist act!


### 3.

Oh if only I could get
    my fourth-grade energy back
                          she told me
         instead of sleeping on cactus pillows
         under wall-hangings of
            children's blots from Nieman-Marcus
and then waking up watching
                    Mean Joe Green on television
                (a sort of Paul Bunyan front-lineman)
   Knock at your own risk
         and duck if you're in the way
      That's
            my philosophy
                          she tittered
            as two too cool young guys
                          saunter in

and sit down at the next table
smoking Luckies and looking around
without expression
and it's Boredom City in their nook
with nothing to do but scratch
And a
Mexican song comes over the juke
blotting out my childhood watching
bored groan-ups sitting around
like wet tortillas

## 4.

While I always dreamed of Afghanistan banana stands
or of opening a roadhouse in Sante Fe
serving blue cheese hamburgers
garlic and scallions on English muffins
with waitresses wearing cactus hats
and electric Navajo blankets
And couples in the booths
in the deep dream department
holding each other's hands
like doves that might fly away
She the most
mindless woman on earth
and he
(muy macho picchu)
a slob from the Avenues
having almost as much fun as if
they were home by themselves
making love every half hour
for three days
and not going out much
after that

## 5.

And then in walks this zingy lady
    I hadn't seen in years
  And a strange sad face she had
        which I hardly recognized
  but she explained it—
      'It's three years later my dear
        and I've been in love
        a few times—
          my head in my cunt
             or close by'
And she really wanted
    the guy at the bar
      but had to leave
        without him
And the men laughed
   and said stuff in Italian
    which they always say
      when women leave bars


And polygamy a tiny village
        in Yucatan


## 6.

But I'm such an optimist
  the *idea* of the Blues
    always eluded me
  even when I met that
      black cattle rancher's wife
    who choked to death
      on a piece of steak

at a party in Santa Fe
while they were listening to
old 45's of Elmore James
who taught them how to treat a black woman
and how to see a black woman
like a  new concept of the Blues


## 7.

When once freaked-out in Ixtlan
the Modesto of Mexico
after taking part in a
group grope
she took a Roar-shack test
while listening to the Ink Spots
and discovered watercolors
painting with her kerchoo tongue
dipped in Quechua ketchup
And one of the weird locals came up
and tried to get sexual again
but she demurred and stated
'Just because Omar Sharif
can play chess
doesn't mean he's Doctor Zhivago
wandering around with leaves
blowing in his face'
And at that very moment
two identical orders of nuns & monks
marched out of the adobe courtyard
chanting 'Liberation Through Masturbation'


## 8.

So back along the Ho Che Men Trail
with Mao or Mouth Say Tongue or Mouse Shoe Tongue

In the famous U.S. Restaurant
   in the last Golden Age of North Beach San Francisco
listening to mafioso conversations
   interlarded with hardrock wingding jabber
by Hong Kong longhair streetgang studs
   with their choppers idling outside
while right-on Red Guards give the finger to
   Chinatown American Legionnaires and sweatshop mothers
with Taiwan real estate men in sharkskin suits
   advancing up the boulevards
leading the Great Chinese Dragon on a string

And the ponderous Italian momma telling me
   "Da bossa no lika da doggie"
when my cockapoolie barked under the table
   at an unbound female foot
And one thousand plastic chopsticks
   dropped straight down thru the peeling ceiling
staking everybody out in their undies
   right where they sat


### 9.

And 'Tennis shoes!' said the seaman disgustedly
   'Tennis shoes! Like this here siren
                         marries the skipper
      and comes on board wearing tennis shoes
      and the crew is so quiet
                     you could hear a fish fart
   and the next thing you know
                   she's painting a tennis court
      on the after deck
         and stringing a net between the stanchions
   and then gets this pussy-whipped skipper
            to throw tennis balls at her

which she bats back at him
           with the Chinese cook playing ballboy
and then when we get out to sea
       with a cargo of tennis balls bound for Wimbledon
            on a sunny day between Scylla and Charybdis
            she's batting balls like that
                   and slams one over the side
      and the racket goes over too
    and she gets the skipper
                      to bring the ship about
      and put two men over the side
                  in a dinghy
    to retrieve the floating capitalist racket
and the two men drown
        and the ship itself runs onto
                        a sawtooth reef
        and goes down with all hands
    as ten thousand tennis balls
                        bob to the surface'


## 10.

'Oh no—Onomatapoeia!'
              cried the poetry workshop teacher
    when she didn't have to pee at all
                   in this Cafesportsevent
        when everyone got up
                  and just for a gas
        read their worst verse
                   (somewhat resembling this)
    —a random colloquial clapping
                        by one hand—
        ten poems burst from it
                        in one night
          tripping on one joint

And that was it
      and so 'Good Night Ladies'
                      he then sang
    as he passed out naked
              (and really *hung*)
     into the adhesive arms
            and slung lips
    of the Strange One

# THE HEAVY

There was this man who was not myself, this short, squat little man, this hunk of meat, this large toad of a man, sitting in the Trieste Café in San Francisco this Saturday noon, in the crowd that comes every Saturday to hear the *padrone* and his son and their friends sing Italian arias, sometimes to jukebox accompaniment and sometimes with a guest guitarist or blind mandolin player, and this noon there is this heavy, silent man sitting by himself at one of the little round tables, you could tell he was alone even though the table was surrounded with sitting people, jammed in, listening to the singing, and he had nothing in particular to attract me to him, he was obviously not attractive, even to women, and he sat there taking it all in, taking long drags on his very long thin *cigarillo*, and every once in a while taking a very small sip of his *cappuccino*, and they were into 'O Solo Mio' when I first noticed him and they were joined in the second chorus by a slender very lovely pale blond woman of maybe thirty-five or a questionable forty, who had a beautiful voice that soared up and away above the young crowd most of which wasn't locals but looked like they'd just come over for the morning on the Sausalito ferry, and this here heavy sitting there like a great hairy sloth or something, and drawing ever so slowly on his long *cigarillo*, holding the smoke so long it never came out anywhere and he so self-contained in the crowd, holding everything in, expressionless, yet watching the singers intently and listening with his large leaden ears which hung in straight black hair tinged with gray which looked like it might be glued to the bottom edge of his bright red felt fedora porkpie hat which he wore perfectly straight on his heavy head, this 'hat' with a life of its own on this head, with a hatband made of very small multi-colored feathers, as in a painting by Leonor Fini, and under this hat came the heavy lids over the heavy eyes behind the heavy lenses in the heavy horned-rims set on a soft-looking blunt nose, directly under which came the thick lips, on each side of which hung the heavy close-shaven jowls with black showing through the skin, and directly under the soft chin came a turtle throat, and then there was the buttoned-in gut in a white leather vest under which were bright red mod pants, and I leaned over and peered for the feet—new bulldog shoes with button hooks! and I contemplated chasing a coin or a hardboiled egg under the table to get a better look at this unbelievable hook-up but the blond singer was into "La Spagnola" and the whole place was humming with pure joy even though life itself was still a tragedy if you lay down, or at least a farce easily turned into a tragedy by sitting upon the ground, and "La Spagnola" proved it all, the sad sweet music pouring out of the lovely mouth of life itself, the parted lips of life, and one had the feeling that this heavy listener spent all his life sitting someplace watching everybody else's life go by, and that he would sit witnessing the most passionate acts of the most beautiful creatures, and show no reaction nor make the slightest gesture beyond the long dragging on his long *cigarillo*, and one could only wonder what bed or lover could possibly have borne him last night, and he was the Mafia godfather of Italian opera out on a scouting tour, and he was James Joyce's Artist, above, beyond, behind the scenes, indifferent, paring his fingernails, and he was a character in a corner of an Egyptian café in Lawrence Durrell's *Justine*, and he was Proust's solitary diner, and he was Dr. Matthew O'Connor in drag in Djuna Barnes' *Nightwood* asking "Watchman, what of the Night?" and he was watching everyone in his Night which was their day, for he was forever an exile in this lighted life, until suddenly a final golden solo came to a glorious climax and everyone clapped and laughed and untangled themselves and spilled out of the café laughing and talking, and the goldenhaired soprano who could have been a *contessa* went straight to *him* and bent over him and kissed him so fully on the lips that he rose up with the lips, and that man and that woman so close they floated out, into the sunlight, together!

33

# GREAT AMERICAN WATERFRONT POEM

San Francisco land's end and ocean's beginning The land the sea's edge also The river within us the sea about us The place where the story ended the place where the story began The first frontier the last frontier Beginning of end and end of beginning End of land and land of beginning Embarcadero Freeway to nowhere turned into part of Vaillancourt's 'Wrecked Freeway Fountain' What is the water saying to the sea on San Francisco waterfront where I spent most of my divorce from civilization in and out waterfront hangouts China Basin Mission Rock Resort Public Fishing Pier Harbor Lunch Tony's Bayview Red's Java House Shanty Gallery Bottom-of-the-Mark Eagle Café Longshoreman's Hall the Waterfront dead No Work No Pay Golden Gate Pilot Boat in fog Podesta Divers SS American Racer rusty Mystic Mariner Motorship Goy Mount Vernon Victory Red Stack Tugs standing out past the pier where I telephoned the lawyers saying I was shipping out on the sailing ship Balclutha and wouldn't be back until they tore down the Embarcadero Freeway along with the rest of petroleum civilization and the literary-industrial complex far from where I'm standing opposite Alcatraz by the thousand fishing boats nested in green thick water The sea a green god feeding Filipino fishermen on the quays Hawaiians in baseball caps and peajackets retired Chief Petty officers casting live bait Puerto Ricans with pile-worms in tincans Old capital N Negroes with catfish called something else here The top of Angel Island showing through fog funneled through Golden Gate Monday morning October sun the Harbor Cruise boat tilting with tourists into a fogbank Gulls on the roofs of piers asleep in sun The Last Mohican eating his lunch out of a pail and catching his next lunch with the last of it The phone booth where I telephoned It's All Over Count Me Out The fog lifting the sun the sun burning through The bright steamers standing out in the end of the first poem I ever wrote in San Francisco twenty years ago just married on a rooftop in North Beach overlooking this place I've come to in this life this waterfront of existence A great view and here comes more life The Western Pacific Freight Ferry ploughing across the horizon between two piers foghorn blowing as I ask a passing elderly ship captain in plaid suit and Tyrolean hat for the time and he takes out his pocket chronometer which says a quarter of two and tells me in thick Norwegian accent "Quarrter to Tvelve' he just off a plane from Chicago no doubt going to catch his ship for the Far East after visiting his aged mother in Minnesota Foghorns still sounding at the Golden Gate An old freighter light-in-the-water on headings adjusting its compass a pilot flag up and the captain on a wing of the bridge coffeemug in hand great-coat collar up The wind beginning to come up blowing the fog away from the phone booth the phone dial very clear All of Angel Island now visible through the fogbank A red hull appears standing-in loaded to the gunnels with oil An Arab on the bridge his turban flying Passing Alcatraz he buys it The Last of the Mohicans reels in his line On the end of it a string of beads once lost in a trade for Manhattan Island The Belt Line Railroad engine stands snorting on a spur next to the Eagle Café with a string of flats & boxcars I park on the tracks imbedded in asphalt and enter the Eagle Café a sign on the wall saying 'Save the Eagle—Last of an Endangered Species' and I get beer just as old brakeman runs in and shouts 'Blue Volkswagen bus!' I rush out and save my bus from the train I see a clock and run for the phone on the pier where the lawyer's supposed to call me back at noon There's a dude in the booth with his address book out and a lot of coins spread out on the ledge He's dialing ten numbers He's putting the coins in very slowly He starts talking slowly He's really enjoying himself The tide is running out The Balclutha strains at its moorings The guy in the booth has a lot to say

**35**

and lotsa time to say it He's in his own civilized world enclosed
in the booth of civilization and I'm in mine outside waiting
for my lawyer to call back with the final word on my divorce
from civilization Will they let Man be free or won't they Will
they or won't they let him be a barbarian or a wanderer if
he wants to I look at my reflection in the glass of the phone
booth outside It's like a mirror of the world with a wild me
in it and the Bank of America towering over behind me Will
Eros or Civilization win And who's this weirdo who is myself
and where does he think he's going to sail away to when
there isn't any longer any Away Another huge oiler stands
in All the fucked-up diplomats of the world on the bridge
holding empty champagne glasses as in a Fellini movie The
guy in the booth hangs up and falls out I sit down in the booth
and drink my beer waiting for the phone to ring The Balclu-
tha's whistle blows The tide is at the ebb The phone rings

# HIGHWAY PATROL

When we zoomed off Freeway 80 other side of Sacramento
and fell into the Old West Motel Coffee Shoppe with the
horseshoe entrance I was wearing my studded cowboy boots
and Stetson hat and my big solid silver deputy star and I
zapped down at the counter and ordered a big ole ranch
breakfast like I could eat a horse and my side-kick he hollered
for soup and fell back to the funky john where I left him in
the stall hoping everything would come out alright heh-heh
and bopped back to the counter past three old dingbats in a
booth talking in some fuckin foreign accent about local real
estate and I got my see-through coffee and the teenybop wait-
ress served up the lukewarm soup and the ranch eggs and
when my buddy escaped from the john he spooned up some
of the lukewarm soup and po-litely noted how it tasted 'real
weird' in fact it was burnt real bad which I pointed out to
the half-ass fry-cook since the waitress had fled and this here
cook comes worrying outa his hole in the wall and mumbles
'Sure as hell is burned, ye can smell it' and I says 'You sure
as hell can, you ole fucker!' as I lit up a Marlboro with a
wood match which I lit with my thumbnail and then we
just whirled around on our stools and took out our po-lice
magnums which we's supposed to carry even off-duty and let
go with a few lil ole blasts right through the ceiling and like
really woke that dump up and everybody got under the tables
and started praying in Swedish or some other goddanged lingo
and my buddy he sauntered up to the jukebox and punched
in a couple selector buttons and give the machine a big jolt
as I punched-in the fry-cook for good measure and the juke
shakes all over and then blasts out so fuckin loud that the
windows blew out and we got blasted right out the door and
everybody come falling out after us and the box just keeps
blasting and the holes in the ceiling we'd shot out is still

smoking and sure as hell they catch fire and the juke itself
catches fire with the Country Western singer still wailing
away like as if his balls done got caught in the meatgrinder
and it's Kell Robertson singing 'I Shot a Faggot in the Bath-
room' and the local volunteer fire department comes sireening
down the highway with antlers on the hood and busts right
in with hard-on hoses and let the whole place have it with
a bath of deer-blood spurting outa their big-ass hose but the
fire kept blazing away in the jumping juke like a redhot
potbelly stove about to blow up and the goddamn roof catches
fire and everybody in sight freaks out and runs off down the
road and over the hill outa sight Man we sure as hell lit that
joint up if you know what I mean All good clean fun and we
died laughin' Just like in the movies

# SEASCAPE WITH SUN & EAGLE

Freer
           than most birds
       an eagle flies high up
                       over San Francisco
                   freer than most places

       soars high up
                   floats and glides high up
           in the still
                   open spaces

               flown from the mountains
                   floated down
                           far over ocean
                       where the sunset has begun
                       a mirror of itself

He sails high over
                   turning and turning
           where seaplanes might turn
           where warplanes might burn

       He wheels about burning
                           in the red sun
               climbs and glides
                   and doubles back
                           upon himself
               now over ocean
                           now over land
                   high over pinwheels stuck in sand
                   where a rollercoaster used to stand

                   soaring eagle setting sun

All that is left of our wildness

## DISSIDENTS, BIG SUR

January bright sun
　　　　　tiny hummingbirds
　　　　　　　　　in the willows
　　　　suddenly
　　　　　　flittering up

　　as an ordinary American monster
　　　　　　　　　fourdoor sedan
　　barrels up the canyon road
　　　backfiring & farting
　　　　　　　　carbon monoxide

And the hummingbirds take flight
　　　　　　in a flurry of fear
　　a cloud of them all at once
　　　　　　　　humming away
　　　　　　　　into deep blue air
　　　where the sky sucks up
　　　　　　　their wingéd hum
　　and in the infinite distance
　　　　　　　　eats them

Even as a crowd of huge defiant
　　　　　　　　upstart crows
　　sets up a ravening raucous
　　　　　　　　*caw ! caw ! caw !*

　　and screams and circles overhead
　　　and pickets the polluted air
　　　　　as the metal monster power-drives
　　　　　on up the canyon
　　　　　and over the horizon

And the crows now too
                    wing away on wind
        and are sucked up
                    and disappear
                            into the omniverous universe

Even as any civilization
                ingests its own most dissident elements

# ALIENATION: TWO BEES

I came upon them in the cabin—
   the angry one at the window
      and the old bent one on the bed
   the one at the window buzzing & buzzing
                  beating its wings on the window
                           beating the pane
      the one on the bed
            the silent one with the bent frame
                     alone on the counterpane
I didn't mean to kill them
   but the one in the window
                  wouldn't be waved
                        back to his hive
         The door was open and he knew it
               and flew in it for a moment
               and then flew back
                        away from his community
Something had alienated him
               and he would not go back
   or was it perhaps
                  the wounded one on the bed
                  who kept him
I tried to get him to fasten onto
                  a crumpled page
                     of the local news
            but he would not
And I must have hurt him doing that
            for he fell on the bed
                  and died in an instant
      stretching out his legs
                  or arms

as if to his comrade or lover
who crawled a quarter-inch toward him
and then hunched up
into a very small furry ball
and was still
and would not move again
As all at once outside
the hive hummed louder
with a million mild conformists
with wild antennas bent

Not one flew out to wake the dead

No messenger was sent

# A VAST CONFUSION

Long long I lay in the sands

Sound of trains in the surf
            in subways of the sea
And an even greater undersound
              of a vast confusion in the universe
     a rumbling and a roaring
                  as of some enormous creature turning
                     under sea & earth
     a billion sotto voices murmuring
              a vast muttering
              a swelling stuttering
       in ocean's speakers
     world's voice-box heard with ear to sand
                  a shocked echoing
                  a shocking shouting
       of all life's voices lost in night
And the tape of it
            somehow running backwards now
    through the Moog Synthesizer of time
                Chaos unscrambled
                   back to the first
                   harmonies

And the first light

## OLBERS' PARADOX

And I heard the learned astronomer
                whose name was Heinrich Olbers
     speaking to us across the centuries
      about how he observed with naked eye
        how in the sky there were
                some few stars close up
    and the further away he looked
                 the more of them there were
    with infinite numbers of clusters of stars
          in myriad Milky Ways & myriad nebulae

So that from this we may deduce
      that in the infinite distances
                there must be a place
                  there *must* be a place
                    where all is light
    and that the light from that high place
                  where all is light
      simply hasn't got here yet
        which is why we still have night

But when at last that light arrives
      when at last it does get here
           the part of day we now call Night
          will have a white sky
             with little black dots in it
             little black holes
                 where once were stars

And then in that symbolic
        so poetic place
           which will be ours
   we'll be our own true shadows
        and our own illumination
               on a sunset earth

## UPON REFLECTION

Night's black mirror is broken

 the star crab has scuttled away

    with the inkwell

     into India

  Dawn

     sows its mustard seed

In the steep ravines and gulches

     of Big Sur

  small animals stir

     under the tough underbrush

as sun creeps down the canyon walls

     into the narrow meadows

  where the wild quail

     run & cluck

  Daytime moon

  after much reflection says

     Sun is God

And the stream

  standing still

     rushes forward

## MATINAL

The critic crow
                struck by the song of

                                morning sun

        has his commentary to make

                                upon it

        stridently

                            *

        dear son

                do not wake

        until I make

                this poem about it

        Then rise & shine
                            It
                                is your world

## DEEP CHESS

Life itself like championship chess
                        dark players jousting
            on a checkered field
                        where you have only
            so much time
                        to complete your moves
And your clock running
                        all the time
            and if you take
                        too much time
                        for one move
            you have that much less
                        for the rest
                        of your life
And your opponent
                        dark or fair
            (which may or may not be
                        life itself)
            picking his nose or yours
            or bugging you with his deep eyes
            or obscenely wiggling his crazy eyebrows
            or blowing smoke in your face
            or crossing and recrossing his legs
                        or her legs
                to reveal a crotch
                        with or without balls
            or otherwise screwing around
            and acting like some insolent invulnerable
                        unbeatable god
            who can read your mind & heart

And one hasty move
                    may ruin you
        for you must play
                    deep chess
          (like the one deep game Spassky won from Fisher)

And if your unstudied opening
                              was not too brilliant
          you must play to win not draw
          and suddenly come up with
                              a new Nabokov variation
And then lay Him out at last
              with some super end-game
                          no one has ever even dreamed of

And there's still time—
                    Your move

# THE RECURRENT DREAM

One of those dreamed landscapes
                    you've dreamt over and over
          with a house you lived in
                        a long time ago
                                    yet never existed
        and a causeway with a bridge
                        which in this latest version
                                        has been taken down
          while you sit eating chocolate almonds
                                            at a party
              in somebody's roofgarden
                                    across the way
              and saying to someone
                            'I used to live
                                    in that house
                                        on the point'
          except that this time
                            the house itself
                                        is gone
      And only the sea's noises
                        with the wood boats knocking
            keeps you from washing away

# A RIVER STILL TO BE FOUND

Stoned &

singing Indian scat

with Ravi Shankar

(as if we knew him)

his sitar like a boat

by the 'river of life'

that flows on & on

into 'eternity'

Time itself a boat

upon that river

Slow distant figures

drawing barges

along those banks

the small drum a pulse

beating slow

under the skin

51

And our bodies

      still in time—

            transported—

dreamt eternal

         by the Ganges—

           a river

          still to be found

          in the interior

        of America

# MONET'S LILIES SHUDDERING

Monet never knew
             he was painting his 'Lilies' for
         a lady from the Chicago Art Institute
             who went to France and filmed
                 today's lilies
                     by the 'Bridge at Giverny'
                         a leaf afloat among them
         the film of which now flickers
             at the entrance to his framed visions
                 with a Debussy piano soundtrack
flooding with a new fluorescence (fleur-essence?)
         the rooms and rooms
                 of waterlilies

Monet caught a Cloud in a Pond
                         in 1903
             and got a first glimpse
                         of its lilies
         and for twenty years returned
             again and again to paint them
                 which now gives us the impression
                     that he floated thru life on them
                             and their reflections
             which he also didn't know
                 we would have occasion
                         to reflect upon

Anymore than he could know
             that John Cage would be playing a
                 'Cello with Melody-driven Electronics'
                         tonight at the University of Chicago
And making those Lilies shudder and shed
                             black light

## INSURGENT MEXICO

In scorched dry desert

where sun is god and god eats life

great god sun going down

pastes up immense red posters

on adobe walls

and then falls down

over the horizon

'with the flare of a furnace blast'

and the posters faded yellow

fall into darkness

leaving only shadows to prove

one more revolution has passed

# A MEETING OF EYES IN MEXICO

Suddenly
you are speaking to me
over the audience
as I speak my poem to it
My eyes encounter yours
over the crowd
Just a pair of eyes out there
in a far foto of faces
distant lamps
in a dark landscape
flickering
And the eyes speak—
in whatever tongue—
The poem ends
The eyes go on
burning
And there is applause out there
as on a dark sea
I hear it distantly
as in a sea shell—
shreds of sunlight blown—
As later your voice comes through—
in whatever tongue—
an impassioned questioning
of my poem—
I answer back
over the heads of the audience

answer you
            Dark eyes
                        speak to you
            over their heads
                        Dark one
'There is none
            like you
                        among the dancers'

            Te amo

# THE GENERAL SONG OF HUMANITY

On the coast of Chile where Neruda lived
   it's well known that
      seabirds often steal
           letters out of mailboxes
             which they would like to scan
              for various  reasons
Shall I enumerate the reasons?
   They are quite clear
      even given the silence of birds
              on the subject
      (except when they speak of it
           among themselves
           between cries)
First of all
     they steal the letters because
        they sense that the General Song
           of the words of everyone
        hidden in these letters
     must certainly bear the keys
       to the heart itself of humanity
           which the birds themselves
             have never been able to fathom
      (in fact entertaining much doubt
       that there actually are
              hearts in humans)
And then these birds have a further feeling
     that their own general song
       might somehow be enriched
         by these strange cries of humans
(What a weird bird-brain idea
    that our titterings might enlighten them)

But when they stole away
                with Neruda's own letters
             out of his mailbox at Isla Negra
        they were in fact stealing back
                     their own Canto General
    which he had originally gathered
                           from them
             with their omniverous & ecstatic
                        sweeping vision
    But now that Neruda is dead
        no more such letters are written
          and they must play it by ear again—
            the high great song
                        in the heart of our blood & silence


*Cuernavaca, October 26, '75*

# EIGHT PEOPLE ON A GOLF COURSE
# AND ONE BIRD OF FREEDOM
# FLYING OVER

The phoenix flies higher & higher
above eight elegant people on a golf course
who have their heads stuck in the sands
of a big trap
One man raises his head and shouts
I am President of Earth. I rule.
You elected me, heh-heh. Fore!
A second man raises his head.
I am King of the Car.
The car is my weapon. I drive all before me.
Ye shall have no other gods.
Watch out. I'm coming through.
A third raises his head out of the sand.
I run a religion. I am your spiritual head.
Never mind which religion.
I drive a long ball. Bow down and putt.
A fourth raises his head in the bunker.
I am the General. I have tanks to conquer deserts.
And my tank shall not want. I'm thirsty.
We play Rollerball. I love Arabs.
A fifth raises his head and opens his mouth.
I am Your Master's Voice.
I rule newsprint. I rule airwaves, long & short.
We bend minds. We make reality to order.
Mind Fuck Incorporated.
Satire becomes reality, reality satire.
Man the Cosmic Joke. Et cetera.
A sixth man raises his gold bald head.
I'm your friendly multinational banker.
I chew cigars rolled with petro-dollars.

We're above nations. We control the control.
I'll eat you all in the end.
I work on margins. Yours.
A woman raises her head higher than anyone.
I am the Little Woman. I'm the Tender Warrior
who votes like her husband. Who took my breasts.
A final figure rises, carrying all the clubs.
Stop or I'll shoot a hole-in-one.
I'm the Chief of All Police. I eat meat.
We know the enemy. You better believe it.
We're watching all you paranoids. Go ahead & laugh.
You're all in the computer. We've got all
your numbers. Except one
unidentified flying asshole.
On the radar screen.
Some dumb bird.
Every time I shoot it down
it rises.

# POPULIST MANIFESTO

Poets, come out of your closets,
Open your windows, open your doors,
You have been holed-up too long
in your closed worlds.
Come down, come down
from your Russian Hills and Telegraph Hills,
your Beacon Hills and your Chapel Hills,
your Mount Analogues and Montparnasses,
down from your foot hills and mountains,
out of your tepees and domes.
The trees are still falling
and we'll to the woods no more.
No time now for sitting in them
As man burns down his own house
to roast his pig.
No more chanting Hare Krishna
while Rome burns.
San Francisco's burning,
Mayakovsky's Moscow's burning
the fossil-fuels of life.
Night & the Horse approaches
eating light, heat & power,
and the clouds have trousers.
No time now for the artist to hide
above, beyond, behind the scenes,
indifferent, paring his fingernails,
refining himself out of existence.
No time now for our little literary games,
no time now for our paranoias & hypochondrias,
no time now for fear & loathing,
time now only for light & love.

We have seen the best minds of our generation
destroyed by boredom at poetry readings.
Poetry isn't a secret society,
It isn't a temple either.
Secret words & chants won't do any longer.
The hour of *om*ing is over,
the time for keening come,
time for keening & rejoicing
over the coming end
of industrial civilization
which is bad for earth & Man.
Time now to face outward
in the full lotus position
with eyes wide open,
Time now to open your mouths
with a new open speech,
time now to communicate with all sentient beings,
All you 'Poets of the Cities'
hung in museums, including myself,
All you poet's poets writing poetry
about poetry,
All you poetry workshop poets
in the boondock heart of America,
All you house-broken Ezra Pounds,
All you far-out freaked-out cut-up poets,
All you pre-stressed Concrete poets,
All you cunnilingual poets,
All you pay-toilet poets groaning with graffitti,
All you A-train swingers who never swing on birches,
All you masters of the sawmill haiku
in the Siberias of America,
All you eyeless unrealists,
All you self-occulting supersurrealists,
All you bedroom visionaries
and closet agitpropagators,

All you Groucho Marxist poets
and leisure-class Comrades
who lie around all day
and talk about the workingclass proletariat,
All you Catholic anarchists of poetry,
All you Black Mountaineers of poetry,
All you Boston Brahmins and Bolinas bucolics,
All you den mothers of poetry,
All you zen brothers of poetry,
All you suicide lovers of poetry,
All you hairy professors of poesie,
All you poetry reviewers
drinking the blood of the poet,
All you Poetry Police—
Where are Whitman's wild children,
where the great voices speaking out
with a sense of sweetness and sublimity,
where the great new vision,
the great world-view,
the high prophetic song
of the immense earth
and all that sings in it
And our relation to it—
Poets, descend
to the street of the world once more
And open your minds & eyes
with the old visual delight,
Clear your throat and speak up,
Poetry is dead, long live poetry
with terrible eyes and buffalo strength.
Don't wait for the Revolution
or it'll happen without you,
Stop mumbling and speak out
with a new wide-open poetry
with a new commonsensual 'public surface'

with other subjective levels
or other subversive levels,
a tuning fork in the inner ear
to strike below the surface.
Of your own sweet Self still sing
yet utter 'the word en-masse'—
Poetry the common carrier
for the transportation of the public
to higher places
than other wheels can carry it.
Poetry still falls from the skies
into our streets still open.
They haven't put up the barricades, yet,
the streets still alive with faces,
lovely men & women still walking there,
still lovely creatures everywhere,
in the eyes of all the secret of all
still buried there,
Whitman's wild children still sleeping there,
Awake and walk in the open air.

# LANDSCAPES OF LIVING & DYING

# THE OLD ITALIANS DYING

For years the old Italians have been dying
all over America
For years the old Italians in faded felt hats
have been sunning themselves and dying
You have seen them on the benches
in the park in Washington Square
the old Italians in their black high button shoes
the old men in their old felt fedoras
                    with stained hatbands
have been dying and dying
                    day by day
    You have seen them
    every day in Washington Square San Francisco
    the slow bell
    tolls in the morning
    in the Church of Peter & Paul
    in the marzipan church on the plaza
    toward ten in the morning the slow bell tolls
    in the towers of Peter & Paul
    and the old men who are still alive
    sit sunning themselves in a row
    on the wood benches in the park
    and watch the processions in an out
    funerals in the morning
    weddings in the afternoon
    slow bell in the morning Fast bell at noon
    In one door out the other
    the old men sit there in their hats
    and watch the coming & going
    You have seen them
    the ones who feed the pigeons
                cutting the stale bread
                    with their thumbs & penknives

the ones with old pocketwatches
the old ones with gnarled hands
                        and wild eyebrows
the ones with the baggy pants
                        with both belt & suspenders
the grappa drinkers with teeth like corn
the Piemontesi the Genovesi the Sicilianos
                smelling of garlic & pepperonis
the ones who loved Mussolini
the old fascists
the ones who loved Garibaldi
the old anarchists reading *L'Umanita Nova*
the ones who loved Sacco & Vanzetti
They are almost all gone now
They are sitting and waiting their turn
and sunning themselves in front of the church
over the doors of which is inscribed
a phrase which would seem to be unfinished
from Dante's *Paradiso*
about the glory of the One
                        who moves everything . . .
The old men are waiting
for it to be finished
for their glorious sentence on earth
                        to be finished
the slow bell tolls & tolls
the pigeons strut about
not even thinking of flying
the air too heavy with heavy tolling
The black hired hearses draw up
the black limousines with black windowshades
shielding the widows
the widows with the long black veils
who will outlive them all
You have seen them

*madre di terra, madre di mare*
The widows climb out of the limousines
The family mourners step out in stiff suits
The widows walk so slowly
up the steps of the cathedral
fishnet veils drawn down
leaning hard on darkcloth arms
Their faces do not fall apart
They are merely drawn apart
They are still the matriarchs
outliving everyone
the old dagos dying out
in Little Italys all over America
the old dead dagos
hauled out in the morning sun
that does not mourn for anyone
One by one Year by year
they are carried out
The bell
never stops tolling
The old Italians with lapstrake faces
are hauled out of the hearses
by the paid pallbearers
in mafioso mourning coats & dark glasses
The old dead men are hauled out
in their black coffins like small skiffs
They enter the true church
for the first time in many years
in these carved black boats
                    ready to be ferried over
The priests scurry about
                as if to cast off the lines
The other old men
                    still alive on the benches
watch it all with their hats on

You have seen them sitting there
waiting for the bocci ball to stop rolling
waiting for the bell
                    to stop tolling & tolling
for the slow bell
                    to be finished tolling
telling the unfinished *Paradiso* story
as seen in an unfinished phrase
                    on the face of a church
as seen in a fisherman's face
in a black boat without sails
making his final haul

## THE SEA AND OURSELVES
## AT CAPE ANN

Caw Caw Caw
on a far shingle long ago
when as a boy I came here
put ear to shell
    of the thundering sea
       sundering sea
   seagulls high over
      calling & calling
    back then
      at Cape Ann Gloucester
Where Olson saw himself Ishmael
 and wrote his own epitaph:
     'I set out now
      in a box upon the sea'
And Creeley found his creel
    yet would not / cd. not
      speak of the sea
And Ferrini took the wind's clothes
  and became the conscience of Gloucester
Yet none could breathe
      a soul into the sea
And I saw the tide pools gasping
  the sea's mouth roaring
       polyphoboistrous
   beyond the Ten Pound Light
      roistering
       off far islands
   'Les Trois Sauvages'
Where Eliot heard
    the sea's stark meditation
  off *beauport* Gloucester

Where I as a man much later
                    made a landfall in the gloaming
        sighting from seaward in convoy
                        beyond the gulls' far off
                                    tattered cries
                cats' cries lost
                    reached to us
                            in shredded snatches
            Then as now
Eliot must
                have been a seaman
                            in his city-soul
        to have heard so deeply
                    the sea's voice sounding then
                            in 'The Dry Salvages'
Here now
            where now
                        is the sea's urge still
        sea's surge and thunder
                            except within us
                    folded under
        by the beach road now
                            rapt in darkness
The sea still a great door never opened
            great ships asunder
                        clinker-built bottoms
                nets hung with cork
                        hulls heavy with caulking
While still the Nor'easter blows
                    still the high tides
                        seethe & sweep shoreward
        batter the breakwaters
                            the granite harbors
                                    rock villages
            Land's End lashed again
                            in 'the sudden fury'

And still the stoned gulls soaring over
                    crying & calling & crying
          blissed-out up there
                              in the darkening air
          over the running sea
                              the runing sea
               over dark stone beach under stars
Where now we sit
                    'distracted from distraction' still
          *Odyssey* turned to *Iliad*
                              in parked cars

# THE MAJESTY

The majesty the sad majesty

           of the universe

                  on grey mornings

     the clouds the furled clouds the grey seas

       like sheets of iron

            Sails on them

       like rusty tin tongues

               struck silent

     vaults of sky shut up

          on huge hinges

      keys thrown away

             into Turner landscapes

'Face of creation' veiled unsmiling

      the waves are mute lips

              curled back

Silence and no answer

        in any 'objective correlative'

     or 'pathetic fallacy'

          The fog

             finds the dumb bell

A dog looks out a port

       daring not to bark

         and tear the veil today

# THE PIED PIPER OF IRON MOUNTAIN

The plane drones toward Iron Mountain Michigan
The sun is setting The seatbelt sign comes on
It is a red dusk We are circling lower
The plane groans as its wheels are lowered
There is a distant rumbling
It is the Iron Mountain opening
On huge sliding hinges
   the side of the mountain
     is sliding open
       with a deep rumbling
The plane is roaring right toward it
I can see its shadow fleeing along the ground
The yawning minehead
        sticks out its black tongue
Smoke pours out
     The roaring grows louder
A small narrow-gauge track
   sticks out the mouth like a bent straw
    disgorging a line of iron-ore cars
Close to the ground now
    our plane lumbers along
      bumping the hot air
I can see huge mills behind us
    great fires glowing red
      blind stacks belching smoke
  blear factories stretched out
       over the plains
    the forges glowing red
      Dark satanic mills!
I look back and see
    myriad trucks and cars
      on the asphalt ground
  all roaring along after us

I take out a small flute
I look down and see myself
I am dressed in a sharp business suit
I have a plastic name-plate on my lapel
I have short hair
                and a pocketful of credit cards
I am clean-shaved with a slight paunch
I have a plastic highball in my hand
My wife is at home with the kiddies
                in the suburbs of Pittsburgh
I have steely blue eyes and a digital wristwatch
I put the flute to my lips and blow
I look back and see
            all our iron progeny
                following me
          riding planes and trucks and trains and cars
The horizon behind us
                is blackened with them
Their smoke obscures the last light
            It may be the year two thousand
Now close ahead
          the black mouth of Iron Mountain
              shudders to receive us
                with a great gnashing
We zoom straight
              through the hot iron gates
The whole bright horde of our children
              roars in after us
And the gates of Iron Mountain
              clang shut


There once was a garden called Earth


Outside in the night
         on the slopes of Iron Mountain
              a great silence descends

The sky cleans itself
               and the stars come out
                              in the total darkness

It is one of those so clear nights
               out on the plains of America
                              when the big sky seems so close
                                             you can touch the stars
It is so quiet
               you can hear
                              the new grass growing

# A NATION OF SHEEP

Flying over the snowfields
of northern Wisconsin
flying low through the Harrisburg fallout
in a twin-engine Cessna
I look down and see
meek cows in the snow
attached to Moo-matic milking machines
tended by Alices in Dairyland
and huge hogs and huge steer
hooked into 'Hot Dog Highways'
producing 36,000 wieners per hour
The beast is fed in by the head
and comes out a dead dog
tongue-tied
The pigs and cows and steer
are all snowed under
as the people are snowed under
by the white rain of laundered news
from government laundries
at Three Mile Island
or wherever the white death breeds
The sky is filled with flocks of sheep
I look down and see the big snow
blanketing the great plains the far prairies
cities lost in it
Perhaps it's Siberia snowed under
with its hydroelectric plant at Zima
But this is not hydro
Here it's ceiling zero
as the snow flies
as Pluto flies
through the skies made of white sheep

Even in Siberia they don't have
such complete snowjobs
The little Cessna flies low
over the socked-in snowfields
It's a late spring silent spring
Flying low I see the fine print
the way you can't see it from high altitudes
on the big official carriers
I look down and see the fine grass roots
the people and cows and pigs
rooting and rutting and dying
feeding and breeding—
Dumb beasts all!
Dumb sheep snowblind
in the white zero snow
the hard white rain
that launders the sky
and falls and falls on the whitened grass
which the cows and pigs and people are eating
as if it were pure light
Even here in Middle America in Middle Earth
even though they know a snowjob when they see one
in the wilds of Wisconsin
or wherever the hard rain falls
they go on swallowing the snow-white lies
following each other head-to-tail
to the dim plutonium shores

*

Still in places not snowbound
in Middle America or Middle Earth
or wherever the hard rain falls

some students some long-hairs some Socratic grey-hairs
still alive in heart and head
are not being snowed
I see them walking with candles
up State Streets to capitols
I see their candles flickering
against the white night
flickering up capitol steps
to the chambers of power wherever
like fireflies everywhere
their candle power everywhere
upon the darkling plain

*(An earlier version of this poem was read by the author and broadcast continuously by an FM station in Madison, Wisconsin, causing candlelight marches and vigils by students at the state capitol during the first week in April 1979.)*

# THE LOVE NUT

I go into the men's room Springfield bus station
on the way back to Muhlenberg County
and see this nut in the mirror
Who let in this weirdo Who let in this creep?
He's the kind writes I LOVE YOU on toilet walls and wants to
　　embrace everybody in the lobby He writes his phone number
　　inside a heart on the wall He's some kinda pervert Mister
　　Eros the Great Lover
He wants to run up to everybody in the waiting room and kiss
　　them on the spot and say Why aren't we friends and lovers
　　Can I go home with you You got anything to drink or smoke
　　Let's you and me get together The time is now or sooner
He wants to take all the stray dogs and cats and people home
　　with him and turn them on to making love all the time
　　wherever
He wants to scatter poems from airplanes across the landscape
　　He's some kinda poetic nut Like he thinks he's Dylan
　　Thomas and Bob Dylan rolled together with Charlie Chap-
　　lin thrown in
He wants to lip-read everybody's thoughts and feelings and
　　longings He's a dangerous nut He's gotta be insane He has
　　no sense of sin
He wants to heat up all the dead-looking people the unhappy-
　　looking people in bus stations and airports He wants to heat
　　up their beds He wants to open their bodies and heads
He's some kinda airhead rolling stone He don't wanna be alone
　　He may be queer on men
He's the kind addresses everybody on buses making them laugh
　　and look away and then look back again

He wants to get everyone to burst out laughing and sighing and crying and singing and dancing and kissing each other including old ladies and policemen

He's gotta be mad He's so glad to be alive he's real strange He's got the hots for humanity one at a time He wants to kiss your breasts He wants to lie still between them singing in a low voice

He wants everyone to lie down together and roll around together moaning and singing and having visions and orgasms He wants to come in you He wants you to come with him He wants us all to come together One hot world One heartbeat

He wants he wants us all to lie down together in Paradise in the Garden of Love in the Garden of Delights and couple together like a train a chain-reaction a chain-letter-of-love around the world on hot nights

He wants he wants he wants! He's gotta be crazy Call the cops Take him away!

# HOLIDAY INN BLUES

In a dark cave called Fuzzy's
                Holiday Inn Spartanburg South Carolina
     some weird ritual being performed
                          by the natives
               a sign proclaiming
'Come Dance the Fuzz Off Your Peaches!'
a country-rock group working out
  an Elvis Presley singer
               bellows at four dim couples dancing
     two of them doing rock-style
                                not touching
                          or looking
                               at each other
               as they thrash about
               as if each were trying
                     to keep his or her balance
     on some erratic highspeed treadmill
The other two couples
                     wrapped around each other
               in the local bear-hug style

When the number is over
                     the dejected-looking couples
          wend their way back to their tables
Two of the men in lumberjack shirts
               shovel the ladies into their seats
          and retreat to their own tables

And the primitive rites continue
                     as two other locals sidle up
          and ask the same middle-age ladies to prance
     as I sit there making up fantastic fictional histories

                    of these two made-up ladies in fancy hair-dos &
                            doubleknit pants suits
One
        I imagine
                    has three grown children in Greenville
                and a fat husband who travels
She has her hair done once a week
                            by a lady barber from Asheville
            who specializes in blue hair & blue gossip
        At her last blue appointment
                    she learned her hubby had been
                            running around with a
                                gay hosiery salesman
                                        in Atlanta
The other lady
                    has never been married but
                                for many years
        has been a receptionist
                            for an elderly dentist
        and has been rumored to have always been
        quite receptive to the dentist
                    whenever he said Open Wide

The cave dance comes to an end again
        and the two ladies slump back to their seats again
        and two more worthies in plaid shirts
            press themselves upon them
            and they're caught again
                            in the bear-hug clutch
                the men hanging onto them
                    as if they were
                            absolutely starved for affection
            on a life-raft somewhere
                clinging to them like life itself
                            or their mothers


                                                        85

yet they are absolute strangers
    returning the ladies to their tables again
with bows and 'thankya m'ams'


The bandleader makes some banter
    about 'them beautiful heffers' he seen on dancefloors
The cave ritual goes on
    as other younger couples struggle up
        and grapple with each other
  as the raunchy singer starts his Buddy Holly numbers
  Three electric guitars with red lights on them
    heat up behind him
    The cave lights glow redder and redder
      the  couples more agitated
        emitting a desperate heat
    The electric fenders clash together
        with showers of sparks
    The drummer speeds up his freight train
    The loudspeakers smoke
        the whole cave rocks
  the writhing couples fall to the floor
    and roll upon each other
      with small passionate cries
    lips clinging to each other
      like suction cups
We've fallen into
    Dante's Inferno
      burning for love
We're trapped inside
    Bosch's Garden of Delights
      groaning with love
We're lost
    in Burroughs' loveless Soft Machine
      with tongues alack
        for love

# CLONING AT THE 'HAWK & DOVE'

I wander into the "Hawk & Dove'
direct from the Library of Congress
Some super-guys and very-together-ladies
                                    at the bar
At the next table I hear a man
                        with a government voice
authoritatively announce to his visitor
that Washington DC is known for one thing
                        the bacon-cheeseburger
Here I'd thought DC was known
        as a seat of some imperial government
Two clones come in
                circle about and land
                        on the other side of me
            both blond California golden boys
                    with hair in their eyes
One says 'I'm starved, man'
            the other 'I'm super-starved!'
They order bacon-cheeseburgers
                    One adds 'Or whatever'
The other pulls out a brochure
                    'Welcome to Washington'
        and stares at it
I am wishing for Ben Shahn's right-angle lens
                    to study their expressions
                        without freaking them out
John Denver comes on the jukebox singing
                    'I'm not half the man
                        I used to be'
One half of a clone or whatever
                        shakes his golden locks
                        off his beardless face
            and catches me
                    eyeballing him

like I'm Priapus
        spying on
                a fertility rite
And I may be born again
my hair turned long and golden
                        a surfboard growing
                                from my feet
And I don't any longer feel
                'like Conrad carrying
                        Coleridge's albatross'


(*The final quotation is taken from Jill Johnston's description of the author in* The Village Voice.)

# THE END OF VARIOUS AFFAIRS

What is that great crow doing
                    flying into my picture
          flying into my various love affairs
                         (with various 'Lenores')
              as if to mark the end
                         of my amores?
This huge black crow floats through
                              the salty air
     and lands on a branch by my window
                         stretching and shaking
                         its dingbat wings
The broken sky above the trees
          has birds for fishes
              in its seas
                    (What waves what rocks what shores!)
While this landlubber crow lets out
                         a great lost cry
          as if to mock the end
                    of my amore
     and louder and louder cries and cries
                         Never never nevermore!

## A SWEET FLYING DREAM

We were two naked
　　　　　light-headed dandelions
　　　　　　　　　　with natural hair blown out
floating high over the landscape
　　　　　　　　　blown by zephyr winds
　　　our long legs dangling
　　　　　　　　　　　　straight down
　　　　　　　translucent
　　　　　　　　　　　　dandelion stems
　　　in an archetypal primordial dream
　　　　　　　　　　　　of flying
Sweet hills & waters
　　　　　　　flowed below us
　　as we floated high over
　　　　　　　　　lakes & rivers
　　　　　　　　　　　　& windblown peaks
We
　　drifted
　　　　　wafted easily
　　　　　　　　　We
　　　　　　　　　　flew wingless
　　Full of air
　　　　　　our hair
　　　　　　　　　buoyed us
We
　　trailed our slim legs
　　　　　　　　in streams of silver air
　　　　　　　There
　　　　　　　　was nothing
　　　　　　　　　　blowing us down
　　　　　　　　or away
　　　　　　　　　　　from each other

After a long way
           and a long while
                      we
                             glided down
                lower & lower
    in great swinging circles
          The sea
               the lapping sea
                      rose up
and we
        were over
               dry gold land
                    close up
  and I
      I was afraid you would
               come against the ground too hard
    and I reached down
            and took
               your two extended hands
                     in mine
    and held you below me
               like that
                  floating
As we drifted
        lower & lower
    the earth
         came up to us
              so softly
And
   we landed
       so quietly
     sank
     so gently
         to the bright soft ground
And lay in the light
        flowerless fields

# TWO SCAVENGERS IN A TRUCK, TWO BEAUTIFUL PEOPLE IN A MERCEDES

At the stoplight waiting for the light
                              Nine A.M. downtown San Francisco
        a bright yellow garbage truck
                              with two garbagemen in red plastic blazers
        standing on the back stoop
                              one on each side hanging on
           and looking down into
                              an elegant open Mercedes
              with an elegant couple in it
The man
              in a hip three-piece linen suit
              with shoulder-length blond hair & sunglasses
The young blond woman so casually coifed
                         with a short skirt and colored stockings
     on the way to his architect's office

And the two scavengers up since Four A.M.
                              grungy from their route
                   on the way home
The older of the two with grey iron hair
                              and hunched back
           looking down like some
                              gargoyle Quasimodo
And the younger of the two
                         also with sunglasses & longhair
        about the same age as the Mercedes driver

And both scavengers gazing down
                              as from a great distance
           at the cool couple

as if they were watching some odorless TV ad
in which everything is always possible

And the very red light for an instant
holding all four close together
as if anything at all were possible
between them
across that great gulf
in the high seas
of this democracy

# THE BILLBOARD PAINTERS

The two
        white-overalled white-capped
                                signpainters
                on the high
                        scaffold suspended
                on the huge
                        billboard
                    beside the elevated
                                freeway
            painting a snapshot landscape of
                        a South Sea island beach
                with lagoon and coral reef and
                                palmtrees
                    thru which the sun
                                is setting and
    the two
            white painters painting a
                            sunburned
                    North American couple on the
                                white beach
            and the real sun cold
                over the myriad flashing cars in
                    the middle of San Francisco
                next to the Hall of questionmark
                                Justice and
    the two
            all-white painters
                            struck motionless with
                arms and paintbrushes raised
                            halfway thru the
                                landscape with
                the right half painted and

                    the left half still blank
                  white on white as if
                        the other half of the world had
                       still to be provided for
                       or as if
                              God or some other
                  slightly less omnipotent
                                    Creator was maybe
                  changing his or her mind half-
                              way thru as if
              even he or she was
                          not so certain anymore it
                        was such a good idea after
                        all
                              to have
        these two so-white All American
                                    painters painting
          that paradise on earth
                        as if
          the advertisers who
                        were paying for this sign
            hadn't already recycled that
                              particular paradise
          with a jet strip and
                        hotels looking like the
              American
                        roman empire where
          they had to advertise now in
              order to fill those fancy
                      wateringplaces with
                              retired billboard
                              painters who
            belonged to the union and
              got themselves and their wives
              all these
                        benefits like

South Sea island trips after
working all their lives in
untropical places like
San Francisco
which
Sir Francis Drake found and
wrote back to the head of *his*
empire saying he
had just discovered
a real unspoiled
native paradise and
if they hurried and
put up billboards back home they
might just be able to
set up a colony out
here with
swimming pools and even maybe make
a pot of gold or
a killing and
die happy in
a beach chair
very far
from home

# HOME HOME HOME

Where are they going
all these brave intrepid animals
Fur and flesh
in steel cabinets
on wheels
high-tailing it
Four PM Friday freeway
over the hidden land
San Francisco's burning
with the late sun
in a million windows
The four-wheeled animals
are leaving it to burn
They're escaping
almost flying
home to the nest
home to the warm caves
in the hidden hills & valleys
home to daddy home to mama
home to the little wonders
home to the pot plants behind the garage
The cars the painted cabinets
streak for home home home
THRU TRAFFIC MERGE LEFT
home to the hidden turning
the hidden yearning
home to San Jose
home to Santa Cruz & Monterey
home to Hamilton Avenue
home to the Safeway the safest way
YIELD
LEFT LANE MUST TURN LEFT

home to the little grey home in the West
home to Granddaddy on the golfcourse
home to Uncle Ned
puttering in the toolshed
having lost his pants
on the stock exchange
home to big sister
who lost her way in encounter groups
home to the 97-1b housewife
driving two tons of chrome & steel
three blocks to the supermarket
to buy a package of baby pins
home to little sister
blushing with boyfriends
in the laundryroom
home to kid brother with skateboards & Adidas
home to mad Uncle building CB radios
in hidden bunkers
home to backyard barbecues
with aerospace neighbors
Mr. Wilson's coming over
The Hendersons will all be there
Home to Hidden Valley
where the widow waits
by the Cross on the mountain
where hangs the true madness
home to Santa's Village
WILL DIVIDE TO SUIT
GAS FOOD LODGING NEXT RIGHT
home to where the food is
home to Watsonville
home to Salinas
past the Grapes of Wrath
past United Farmworkers

stooped over artichokes
home home over the horizon
where the sun still blows
into the sea
home to Big Sur
and the garden of delights
and the oranges of Hieronymous Bosch
the sun still sets
in lavender skies
Home sweet home the salesman sighs
home safe at home in the bathroom
safe with the washingmachine & dishwasher
safe with the waterheater
safe with the kitchen clock
tick tick
the time is not yet
the alarm is set
safe at last in the double bed
hidden from each other
in the dark bed by the winding stair
the enchanted place in the still air
hidden each from each
or the queensize bed the kingsize bed
the waterbed with the vibrator
with the nylon nympho in it
the bed of roses
the bed with Big Emma in it
with the stoned-out Angel in it
(Mountains of flesh
Hills of hips & thighs
Rolling landscapes of heaving meat
Groans & moans & cries!)
Home to the bed we made
and must lie in

with 'whoever'
Or home to the bed still to be made
of ragas & visions
the bed whose form is pure light
(and unheard melodies
dark despairs & inchoate ecstasies
longings out of reach)
Who to decipher them who answer them
singing each to each?
Hidden from themselves
The beds are warm with them
The springs quake
on the San Andreas Fault
The dark land broods
Look in my eye, look in my eye
the cyclope tv cries
It blinks and rolls its glassy eye
and shakes its vacuum head
over the shaken bodies
in the bed

# SAN JOSE SYMPHONY RECEPTION
(*Flagrante delicto*)

The bald man in plaid playing the harpsichord
    stopped short and sidled over
                    to the sideboard
     and copped a piece of Moka
             on a silver plate
     and slid back and started playing again
       some kind of Hungarian rhapsodate
    while the lady with the green eyeshades
      leaned over him exuding
                admiration & lust
Half notes danced & tumbled
              out of his instrument
     exuding a faint odor of
         chocolate cake
In the corner I was taking
        a course in musical destruction
  from the dark lady cellist
     who bent over me with her bow unsheathed
     and proceeded to saw me in half
As a consequence my pants fell right off
    revealing a badly bent trombone which
     even the first flutist
       who had perfect embouchure
           couldn't straighten out

101

# WHITE ON WHITE

Today I'll write white on white
wear nothing but white
drink nothing but white
eat nothing but white
And I would be that sea-creature
who eats light
straining the ocean for its phosphorous—
For present time
is a 'white dot' in space
and white is the sand
in the hourglass
running out
White dunes of Africa
running through it
Snows of Siberia
sifting through it
The seas white with sperm
under the white moon
where aluminum stars wheel about
noiselessly
over quivering earth
with its white whales
white phagocytes
white bleached skulls
and albino animals
(Blacks bleached out
into white men?)
And to dream of white string
a symbol of innocence
Though the color of death be white
And the world checkered with death
white-on-black & black-on-white

'dumb pawns
in black-and-white kingdoms'
An angel stands on a station platform
slowly shaking its gossamer wings
A white horse
comes alone from a torn village
Everywhere around the earth
on station platforms they
are still putting up the placards
*No pasaran*
Go back Wrong way
White searchlights
search the sky
The gun turrets turn
on the old Walls
The angel slowly moves its wings
breathing the light white air
The earth breathes and trembles with it
The governed
will be governed
Liberty is not freedom
Eros versus civilization
No Way
without a pass
It is snowing white documents
The very rich
get richer still
A white gloved hand
still reaches out the window
for the money in the cup
Liberty is not free
The angel
stands on the edge
of the station platform

slowly moving its large white wings
which look too fragile
to lift the body of being
which still breathes anarchist air
And the train
the train made of nothing but boxcars
jammed with three billion people
still stands in the station trembling
And white phoenixes arise
out of piñon smoke
And the 'white sphinx of chance'
still holds its tongue
on the desert roads of the future

# AN ELEGY TO DISPEL GLOOM

*(After the assassinations of Mayor George Moscone and Supervisor Harvey Milk in San Francisco, November, 1978)*

Let us not sit upon the ground
and tell sad stories
of the death of sanity.
That two sweet men are dead
is all that need be said.
Two such sentient beings
two humans made of flesh
are meshed in death
and no more need be said.
It is pure vanity
to think that all humanity
be bathed in red
because one young mad man
one so bad man
lost his head.
The force that through the red fuze
drove the bullet
does not drive everyone
through the City of Saint Francis
where there's a breathless hush
in the air today
a hush at City Hall
and a hush at the Hall of Justice
a hush in Saint Francis Wood
where no bird
tries to sing
a hush on the Great Highway
and in the great harbor
upon the great ships

and on the Embarcadero
from the Mission Rock Resort
to the Eagle Cafe
a hush on the great red bridge
and on the great grey bridge
a hush in the Outer Mission
and at Hunter's Point
a hush at a hot potato stand on Pier 39
and a hush at the People's Temple
where no bird
tries its wings
a hush and a weeping
at the Convent of the Sacred Heart
on Upper Broadway
a hush upon the fleshpots
of Lower Broadway
a pall upon the punk rock
at Mabuhay Gardens
and upon the cafes and bookstores
of old North Beach
a hush upon the landscape
of the still wild West
where two sweet dudes are dead
and no more need be said.
Do not sit upon the ground and speak
of other senseless murderings
or worse disasters waiting
in the wings
Do not sit upon the ground and talk
of the death of things beyond
these sad sad happenings.
Such men as these do rise above
our worst imaginings.

# ADIEU À CHARLOT

*(Second Populist Manifesto)*

Sons of Whitman sons of Poe
sons of Lorca & Rimbaud
or their dark daughters
poets of another breath
poets of another vision
Who among you still speaks of revolution
Who among you still unscrews
the locks from the doors
in this revisionist decade?
'You are President of your own body, America'
Thus spoke Kush in Tepotzlan
youngblood wildhaired angel poet
one of a spawn of wild poets
in the image of Allen Ginsberg
wandering the wilds of America
'You Rimbauds of another breath'
sang Kush
and wandered off with his own particular paranoias
maddened like most poets
for one mad reason or another
in the unmade bed of the world
Sons of Whitman
in your 'public solitude'
bound by blood-duende
'President of your own body America'
Take it back from those who have maddened you
back from those who stole it
and steal it daily
The subjective must take back the world
from the objective gorillas & guerrillas of the world
We must rejoin somehow

the animals in the fields
in their steady-state meditation
'Your life is in your own hands still
Make it flower make it sing'
(so sang mad Kush in Tepotzlan)
'a constitutional congress of the body'
still to be convened to seize control
of the State
the subjective state
from those who have subverted it
The arab telephone of the avant-garde
has broken down
And I speak to you now
from another country
Do not turn away
in your public solitudes
you poets of other visions
of the separate lonesome visions
untamed uncornered visions
fierce recalcitrant visions
you Whitmans of another breath
which is not the too-cool breath of modern poetry
which is not the halitosis of industrial civilization
Listen now Listen again
to the song in the blood the dark duende a dark singing
between the tickings of civilization
between the lines of its headlines
in the silences between cars
driven like weapons
In two hundred years of freedom
we have invented
the permanent alienation of the subjective
almost every truly creative being
alienated & expatriated
in his own country

in Middle America or San Francisco
the death of the dream in your birth
o meltingpot America
I speak to you
from another country
another kind of blood-letting land
from Tepotzlan the poets' lan'
Land of the Lord of the Dawn

                              Quetzalcoatl

Land of the Plumed Serpent
I signal to you
as Artaud signaled
through the flames
I signal to you
over the heads of the land
the hard heads that stand like menhirs
above the land in every country
the short-haired hyenas
who still rule everything
I signal to you from Poets' Land
you poets of the alienated breath
to take back your land again
and the deep sea of the subjective
Have you heard the sound of the ocean lately
the sound by which daily
the stars still are driven
the sound by which nightly
the stars retake their sky
The sea thunders still to remind you
of the thunder in the blood
to remind you of your selves
Think now of your self
as of a distant ship
Think now of your beloved
of the eyes of your beloved

whoever is most beloved
he who held you hard in the dark
or she who washed her hair by the waterfall
whoever makes the heart pound
the blood pound
Listen says the river
Listen says the sea Within you
you with your private visions
of another reality a separate reality
Listen and study the charts of time
Read the sanskrit of ants in the sand
You Whitmans of another breath
there is no one else to tell
how the alienated generations
have lived out their expatriate visions
here and everywhere
The old generations have lived them out
Lived out the bohemian myth in Greenwich Villages
Lived out the Hemingway myth
in *The Sun Also Rises*
at the Dôme in Paris
or with the bulls at Pamplona
Lived out the Henry Miller myth
in the *Tropics* of Paris
and the great Greek dream
of *The Colossus of Maroussi*
and the tropic dream of Gauguin
Lived out the D. H. Lawrence myth
in *The Plumed Serpent*
in Mexico Lake Chapala
And the Malcolm Lowry myth
*Under the Volcano* at Cuernavaca
And then the saga of *On the Road*
and the Bob Dylan myth Blowing in the Wind
How many roads must a man walk down

How many Neal Cassadys on lost railroad tracks
How many replicas of Woody Guthrie with cracked guitars
How many photocopies of longhaired Joan
How many Ginsberg facsimiles and carbon-copy Keseys
still wandering the streets of America
in old tennis shoes and backpacks
or driving beat-up school buses
with destination-signs reading 'Further'
How many Buddhist Catholics how many cantors
chanting the Great Paramita Sutra
on the Lower East Side
How many Whole Earth Catalogs
lost in out-houses on New Mexico communes
How many Punk Rockers waving swastikas
Franco is dead but so is Picasso
Chaplin is dead but I'd wear his bowler
having outlived all our myths but his
the myth of the pure subjective
the collective subjective
the Little Man in each of us
waiting with Charlot or Pozzo
On every corner I see them
hidden inside their tight clean clothes
Their hats are not derbys they have no canes
but we know them
we have always
waited with them
They turn and hitch their pants
and walk away from us
down the darkening road
in the great American night

*(Tepotzlan '75—San Francisco '78)*

# LOOK HOMEWARD, JACK:
## TWO CORRESPONDENCES

### 1.

Cruising down long winding highway near Asheville and look-ing East over vast high plain stretched way below Blue Ridge horizon—from high on that highway coming down and round a bend and seeing rapt panorama laid out like the *altoplano* of Tenochtitlan, ancient Aztec Mexico as I saw it coming down past Popocatepetl from the West and Tepotz'lan—the old Aztec capitol there spread out before Cortez under the verdant forest—jungle-like rich deep blue-green woods and fields running to the horizon like some blue-green sea—the whole Aztec civilization alive there hidden under the lush green canopy—a Kerouac vision of the great fellaheen metropole, how it must have looked to a rider coming sudden upon it from the far side of Popo, some great warrior on horseback, stoned on peyotl, with gold head-piece and flashing sword, staring down at the sleeping hidden huge island city in early morn—All gone now, Tenochtitlan buried under. . . . Mexico City Blues! In the American grain. . . .

## 2.

In the Thomas Wolfe boardinghouse in Asheville . . . rooms he slept in . . . typewriter he once used . . . his books and clothes and photos . . . one early photo looking exactly like a young Jack Kerouac—set me musing, high on Mexican grass—Sweeping vision of America in *Look Homeward, Angel*, seen by the young Eugene Gant as he rode a train through the American dusk—'to flash upon the window and be gone'—Wolfe's place, said Maxwell Perkins, was all America—So with Jack—Kerouac's vision a car vision, seen from windows of old autos speeding cross-country—the same Wolfian old pre-War America, now all but gone, invisible, except in Greyhound bus stations in small lost towns. . . . And Jack's Lowell, Mass., a mill town and Asheville like a mill town after the mills moved South early in the century, carrying Canuck ghosts with them. . . . Wolfe and Jack drinking together now in eternity . . . omniverous insatiable consumers, of life, which consumed them both too early. . . . Wolfe's stone angel akin to Jack's stone Stations of the Cross in Lowell graveyard, angels of mercy. . . . Both never happy abroad, never happy expatriates—Wolfe drunk in Berlin, Jack stoned on a Mexican rooftop or staggering by the Seine. . . . And which of them would know his brother? . . . Look Homeward, Jack.

# FROM 'NORTHWEST ECOLOG'

## THE OLD SAILORS

On the green riverbank
                        age late fifties
I am beginning
                to remind myself
of my great Uncle Désir
                    in the Virgin Islands
On a Saint Thomas back beach
he lived when I last saw him
in a small shack
                  under the palms
Eighty years old
                  straight as a Viking
  (where the Danes once landed)
he stood looking out
                   over the flat sea
  blue eyes or grey
                with the sea in them
salt upon his lashes
              We
         were always sea wanderers
No salt here now
            by the great river
  in the high desert range
Old sailors stranded
        the steelhead
          they too lost without it
                    leap up and die

## WILD LIFE CAMEO, EARLY MORN

By the great river Deschutes
          on the meadowbank greensward
    sun just hitting
            the high bluffs
     stone cliffs sculpted
             high away
      across the river

At the foot of a steep brown slope
             a mile away
    six white-tail deer
  four young bucks with branched antlers
    and two small does
            mute in eternity
              drinking the river
then in real time raising heads
    and climbing up and up
            a steep faint switchback
     into full sun

I bring them close in the binoculars
            as in a round cameo
   There is a hollow bole in a tree
              one looks into
  One by one they
        drink silence
           (the two does last)
    one by one
        climb up so calm
            over the rim of the canyon
    and without looking back
            disappear forever

Like certain people
     in my life

115

# CLAMSHELL ALLIANCE

Here by the sea
                        Vashon Island Puget Sound
          at the Portage
                              lie in bed
                                        thinking what to do
'The sea
          is calm tonight'
Beneath it
          all not so calm
Nor inside us
                    here at this isthmus
          this portage
                        between two lives
          this isthmus
                          built on Indian arrowheads
          all not so calm
We are all
              submerged in our lives
                              in the 'bath of creation'
Yet the tide is full
The small clams and Quilcene oysters
                        are their own alliance
                                against the world's death
They are in league
                  with the seas and the whales
They are in league
                  with Moby Dick
                        against the Ahabs of earth
The clams
            live and breathe closed up
We too
        close up tight on shore
                            clam up

Yet here by the sea
                on Vashon
                            may open out
        in this summerhouse
                            as in a small Maine seaport
        or wherever—
                    Vashon or Mannahatta—
        the same salt tongue
                        licks us all
The stinging salt
        if we should open up
                        pours in
        but also the light
                        the lapped light of love. . .
        An illusion by the sea?
                            a romantic agony?
            a faint flickering
                        in the gloaming?
    At the Coast Guard station
                    the great white lighthouse
                            still flashes all ways

# READING APOLLINAIRE BY THE ROGUE RIVER

Reading Apollinaire here
sitting crosslegged
on sleepingbag & poncho
in the shadow of a huge hill
before the sun clears it
Woke up early on the shore
and heard the river shushing
(like the sound a snake might make
sliding over riprap
if you magnified the sound)
My head still down upon the ground
one eye without perspective
sees the stream sliding by
through the sand
as in a desert landscape
Like a huge green watersnake
with white water markings
the river slithers by
and where the canyon turns
and the river drops from sight
seems like a snake about to disappear
down a deep hole
Indians made their myths
of this great watersnake
slid down from mountains far away
And I see the Rogue for real
as the Indians saw him
the Rogue all wild white water
a cold-blooded creature
drowning and dousing
the Rogue ruler of the land
transforming it at will
with a will of its own

a creature to be feared and respected
pillaging its way to the sea
with great gravity
still ruled by that gravity
which still rules all
so that we might almost say
Gravity is God
manifesting Himself
as Great God Sun
who will one day make Himself
into a black hole in space
who will one day implode Himself
into Nothing
All of which the slithering Rogue
knows nothing of
in its headlong
blind rush to the sea
And though its head
is already being eaten
by that most cruel and churning
monster Ocean
the tail of the snake
knows it not
and continues turning & turning
toward its final hole
and toward that final black hole
into which all some day
will be sucked burning

As I sit reading a French poet
        whose most famous poem is about
                the river that runs through the city
                        taking time & life & lovers with it
                                And none returning
                                        none returning

# ROUGH SONG OF ANIMALS DYING

In a dream within a dream I dreamt a dream
of the reality of existence
inside the ultimate computer
which is the universe
in which the Arrow of Time
flies both ways
through bent space
In a dream within a dream I dreamt a dream
of all the animals dying
all animals everywhere
dying & dying
the wild animals the longhaired animals
winged animals feathered animals
clawed & scaled & furry animals
rutting & dying & dying
In a dream within a dream I dreamt a dream
of creatures everywhere dying out
in shrinking rainforests
in piney woods & high sierras
on shrinking prairies & tumbleweed mesas
captured beaten strapped starved & stunned
cornered & traded
species not meant to be nomadic
wandering rootless as man
In a dream within a dream I dreamt a dream
of all the animals crying out
in their hidden places
in the still silent places left to them
slinking away & crawling about
through the last wild places
through the dense underbrush
the last Great Thickets
beyond the mountains

crisscrossed with switchbacks
beyond the marshes
beyond the plains & fences
(the West won with barbed-wire machines)
in the high country
in the low country
crisscrossed with highways
In a dream within a dream I dreamt a dream
of how they feed & rut & run & hide
In a dream within a dream I saw
how the seals are beaten on the ice-fields
the soft white furry seals with eggshell skulls
the Great Green turtles beaten & eaten
exotic birds netted & caged & tethered
rare wild beasts & strange reptiles & weird woozoos
hunted down for zoos
by bearded blackmarketeers
who afterwards ride around Singapore
in German limousines
In a dream within a dream I dreamt a dream
of the earth heating up & drying out
in the famous Greenhouse Effect
under its canopy of carbon dioxide
breathed out by a billion
infernal combustion engines
mixed with the sweet smell of burning flesh
In a dream within a dream I dreamt a dream
of animals calling to each other
in codes we never understand
The seal and steer cry out
in the same voice
as they are clubbed
in Chicago stockyards & Newfoundland snowfields
It is the same cry
The wounds never heal

in the commonweal of animals
We steal their lives
to feed our own
and with their lives
our dreams are sown
In a dream within a dream I dreamt a dream
of the daily scrimmage for existence
in the wind-up model of the universe
the spinning meat-wheel world
in which I was a fish who eats his tail
in which I was a claw upon a beach
in which I was a snake upon a tree
in which I was a serpent's egg
a yin-yang yolk of good and evil
about to consume itself

# HORSES AT DAWN

The horses the horses the wild horses at dawn
as in a watercolor by Ben Shahn
they are alive in the high meadow
in the high country on the far mesa
you can see them galloping
you can see them snorting
you can hear their thunder distantly
you can hear the small thunder
of their small hooves
insistently
like wood hammers thrumming
on a distant drum
The sun roars &
throws their shadows
out of the night

BIBLIOGRAPHICAL NOTES & CREDITS

## WHO ARE WE NOW?

The publication history of "Populist Manifesto" is extraordinary: An early version was broadcast by the author on KPFA/FM (Berkeley) in April 1975. On April 23, he spoke it at Walt Whitman Day, Rutgers University (Camden). Its first appearance in print, like an early election return, was in a small town paper in New Hampshire, the *Granite State Independence* (Grantham, N.H.) in May 1975, followed closely by the Bolinas (California) *Hearsay News*. It was picked up by the *Los Angeles Times* on June 1, by *The New York Times* (Op/Ed page) on July 5, and by the *San Francisco Examiner* on August 10, 1975. (Apologies are due to the *American Poetry Review*, which had the poem set in type when it appeared in *The New York Times*.) A flood of publication in literary magazines followed: *The Chicago Review, California State Poetry Quarterly, Nitty Gritty* (Pasco, Washington), *Sol Tide* (New Mexico), and more informal mimeo places, since the author gave it to anyone who asked. . . . Within a half-year of its first publication, it also was translated into Spanish, Italian, French, and published in the anarchist *Antigruppo 1975* (Sicily) and *Impegno 70* (Sicily), and the *Revista de Bellas Artes* #23 (Mexico City). Its first publication in England was in *Z-revue Collective* (Leicester), and it was pirated in Yugoslavia. A broadside of it was printed by Vernon Chadwick, Jr. at the Cranium Press (San Francisco) and reprinted later by City Lights Books. New Directions printed it in its anthology *ND31*. And the late jazz critic Ralph Gleason, in one of his last acts, wrote to Jann Wenner, editor of *Rolling Stone*, urging him to publish it as "an important literary document of the '70s." Thanks are due also to the following publications in which other poems herein first were printed: *The New York Times, Beatitude Magazine, Poetry Now, City of San Francisco, Los Angeles Times, San Francisco*

*Examiner, Chicago Review, California State Poetry Quarterly, Revista de Bellas Artes, Transatlantic Review, San Francisco Bay Guardian, Bastard Angel, Pacific Sun Literary Quarterly, The CoEvolution Quarterly*, and various *New Directions in Prose and Poetry* anthologies.

## LANDSCAPES OF LIVING AND DYING

"The Old Italians Dying" first was published in the *Los Angeles Times*. "The Sea and Ourselves at Cape Ann" was printed first in *The New York Times Magazine*, September 11, 1977. "A Nation of Sheep" appeared in *The New York Times*, May 12, 1979. "Two Scavengers in a Truck . . ." and "The Billboard Painters" appeared in the *Los Angeles Times*, November 12, 1978, the latter also in the *San Francisco Chronicle and Examiner*, as did "Home Home Home." "White On White," issued as a broadside by the Committee on the Breytenbach Case, also appeared in the *Co-Evolution Quarterly* (Fall 1978). "Adieu à Charlot" was in the *Los Angeles Times*, March 5, 1978, *San Francisco Examiner, City Lights Journal #4*, and *New Directions #38*, and was also printed as broadsides by the Lawton Press (New Rochelle, N.Y.) and White Wail Press (San Francisco). It has been translated and published in France, Germany, and Italy. "An Elegy to Dispel Gloom" came out in the *San Francisco Examiner*, November 29, 1978. Poems from *Northwest Ecolog* are taken from the City Lights Book (1978). "Reading Apollinaire by the Rogue River" was first in the *Los Angeles Times*, October 23, 1977.

# INDEX OF TITLES AND FIRST LINES

127

# New Directions Paperbooks—A Partial Listing

For complete listing request free catalog from
New Directions, 80 Eighth Avenue, New York 10011          †Bilingual

For complete listing request free catalog from
New Directions, 80 Eighth Avenue, New York 10011

†Bilingual